Being Happy

The Sacred Art of Letting Go and Letting God

With much
more ♥ happiness ☺
Anne

Anne K. Ross

BALBOA.
PRESS

A DIVISION OF HAY HOUSE

Balboa Press books may be ordered through booksellers or by contacting:

Balboa Press
A Division of Hay House
1663 Liberty Drive
Bloomington, IN 47403
www.balboapress.com
1 (877) 407-4847

Because of the dynamic nature of the Internet, any web addresses or links contained in this book may have changed since publication and may no longer be valid. The views expressed in this work are solely those of the author and do not necessarily reflect the views of the publisher, and the publisher hereby disclaims any responsibility for them.

The author of this book does not dispense medical advice or prescribe the use of any technique as a form of treatment for physical, emotional, or medical problems without the advice of a physician, either directly or indirectly. The intent of the author is only to offer information of a general nature to help you in your quest for emotional and spiritual well-being. In the event you use any of the information in this book for yourself, which is your constitutional right, the author and the publisher assume no responsibility for your actions.

Any people depicted in stock imagery provided by Thinkstock are models, and such images are being used for illustrative purposes only. Certain stock imagery © Thinkstock.

Print information available on the last page.

ISBN: 978-1-5043-5521-6 (sc)
ISBN: 978-1-5043-5522-3 (e)

Balboa Press rev. date: 5/11/2016

In Gratitude

This book would never have made it to where it is, published, without a few talented people. I would like to acknowledge Debra Sampson Boogaard, a developmental editor, for assisting me on my journey with constructive collaboration. My front cover artwork was created by a very talented, though modest artist, who by day manages people and money, my son-in-law, Trevor Woods. And, last but definitely not least, to my husband and children, who have endured my relentless insights and teachings, and continue to love and support me through this never ending journey. Blessings to you all and I thank you dearly.

Disclaimer

The information provided in this book is designed to provide helpful information on the subjects discussed. This book is not meant to be used, nor should it be used, to diagnose or treat any medical condition. For diagnosis or treatment of any medical problem, consult your own physician. The author is not responsible for any specific health needs that may require medical supervision and are not liable for any damages or negative consequences from any treatment, action, application or preparation, to any person reading or following the information in this book. References are provided for informational purposes only and do not constitute endorsement of any websites or other sources. I am not a licensed physician, psychoanalyst, or therapist. If you feel you need medical attention, please seek a licensed professional doctor.

In this book I make reference to God/Source/Spirit. These are the words that, in general, best describes what I believe to be my driving force: a power, an energy, a voice. I am not discrediting any religion or term, and my writing is not meant to devalue anyone's beliefs or religious affiliation. My belief is based on unconditional love for self, other, animal, the earth, and the greater good of all.

Chapter 1

My Intention for This Book

The meaning of life is to find your gift.
The purpose of life is to give it away.

—Pablo Picasso

The intention for this book came about after I delivered a presentation to a group of certified public accountants, introducing toys that would empower them to more effectively interact with clients, staff, and other key relationships. The presentation was based upon my personal experience in our own CPA practice. I realized that other CPAs could benefit from the toys that I had implemented, and they could enjoy more successful daily lives.

After delivering this presentation at the CPAmerica International conference in Chicago, Illinois, in October 2014, I recognized that the application of these toys could benefit everyone in any aspect of his or her life. These are the toys that I use and have incorporated into my coaching. They may be of benefit to you if you are seeking to advance your understanding of your true self, find your life's purpose and desires, achieve financial success, empower relationships, or continue on your path of deeper self-discovery.

My intention for this book is to provide you with toys that assist you on your path toward cultivating and managing relationships with yourself and others, becoming more in tune with your feelings and intuition, and exploring your true purpose. These toys are meant as jump-starters as you embark or continue on your life journey. You may be at a point in your life where you want to continue your self-discovery with some guided coaching. Wherever you are at is where you are supposed to be. Simply breathe and know that this book will help you on your way.

My offering to you is this: Be open when you read through the book. After you have completed the reading, take time to sift through the toys and pick out what resonates with you. Try them out; play with them for a while. Breathe and give yourself and the toys some time to notice the benefits.

Chapter 2

My Story

Your time is limited; don't waste it living someone else's life. Don't be trapped by dogma, which is living with the result of other peoples' thinking. Don't let the noise of others' opinions drown out your own inner voice. And, most important, have the courage to follow your heart and intuition. They somehow know what you truly want to become. Everything else is secondary.

—Steve Jobs

There's always a beginning, an impetus to what is the inspiration behind an experience or event. My story was the impetus for my inspiration to become a coach.

As the youngest of three children, I was born into a loving family. My parents were high school sweethearts. Unexpectedly, my father transitioned (passed away) when he was thirty-two, leaving my mother with three children under the age of five. Uncertainty led my mother to remarry, and our lives changed.

My father had been a loving and strong figure in my young life. As I grew, I faced negative experiences, and his absence left me without the wise, positive, supportive messages that otherwise would have served as buffer and counterbalance to the negative messages I received. As I matured, I started to believe certain things were true about me and my life based on how I felt. *I created those beliefs.* My feelings were my indicators that I was either good or bad and that certain things in my life were good or bad. All of these experiences, thoughts, feelings, and beliefs were mine. No one made me think, feel, or believe any of them. I created them.

In some psychology, it is believed that immediate family/ caregivers influence a child's belief system. My belief is that although this may be the dominate belief; I strongly believe that everyone has the power and ability to reprogram themselves to learn their own truth, their beliefs for their greater good.

Despite negative messages I received from some people I encountered, I knew deep down that I was inherently a good person. For the life of me, I couldn't figure out why anyone could think otherwise. Yet life gave me experiences, thoughts, and feelings that didn't appear to agree with my concept of myself as an inherently good person. I knew that my understanding of this concept, was the truth—my truth.

I also felt an external force that was much bigger than me. It couldn't be seen; it was a sense that I had received, in an unspoken message, a truth beyond me. I thought everyone had that same feeling or understanding. I vividly remember being a young child out in nature when this sense, this feeling, came over me that conveyed, "Everything is going to be okay. You will be taken care of." It was as if a big, booming voice bestowed this gift on me. Yet there was no sound, no distinct tone. It seemed to be everywhere outside of me, and it deeply penetrated my being. That statement became my anchor. I was so relieved the message of my truth confirmed my natural initial belief. I felt safe about the present and the future. A peace and calm transcended me.

Since then, I've honed in on my feelings, which inspired my curiosity to find out what it all meant. I began to dive deeply, to question my thoughts and beliefs, and to educate myself. I began to ask a lot of questions over a period of years, starting when I was twelve years old.

Why is such a great start, don't you agree? This has been a lifelong journey that eventually led me to become a certified spiritual life coach so that I could assist others on their journeys. I feel so passionate when I'm coaching and helping others. I had many horrible experiences in my early life. However, I'm ever so grateful for those experiences because they have led me to know that I've found my purpose, my calling.

It's so exciting when I'm sharing, coaching, and offering my services. That's how I know others can achieve this same feeling while finding their purpose, getting unstuck, finding love relationships, deepening relationships, achieving better health, and creating abundant lives. I've lived it and know that this is my truth.

In my role as a spiritual life coach, I create trust. My clients feel safe and protected while they explore their lives and experiences to discover their authentic selves and true callings.

One of my philosophies is that we all want to feel loved, accepted, and validated; we all want to have a safe and trusted place where we can be who we are meant to be. It's when we're living our true life's purpose that we will be filled with joy, achieve optimal health, receive greater abundance, and develop empowered relationships.

My coaching is a collaborative win–win for my clients and me. This is where true happiness lives, and I desire happiness for you.

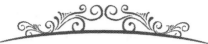

Chapter 3

Being Happy

Appreciate what is, be eager for what is coming,
and know that there is great love for you here.

—Abraham-Hicks

We're meant to be happy all of the time. When did we get so serious about ourselves and life? Look at small children: they're usually joyous, happy, playful, creative, silly, and spontaneous. Those are characteristics we're supposed to maintain all of the time. As long as you're not hurting yourself or others, be childlike.

Being childlike all of the time is our purpose; it's what God/Source/Spirit wants for us. You may have forgotten how to be childlike, and that's okay. We're all on our own unique paths. The world is waiting for you, not a copy of someone else. As Marianne Williamson, author of *A Return to Love*, advocates, your playing small doesn't serve anyone, least of all yourself.

Just for fun, sit for a moment and reflect on something that made you smile, that made you instantly happy as a child. Remember? It's freeing, and there are no conditions about it that required you to be happy.

What gave you joy as a child may not be the same things that give you joy now. Think of something that instantly gives you joy and contentment, with no conditions. Breathe, relax, and ponder this for a few minutes. Be at peace with the process.

The purpose of this exercise is to become aware. Awareness is key for personal growth and self-realization. Become aware of how you feel; there are no right or wrong answers. Examine a thought, feeling, or belief and decide whether it's serving your greater good. If not, say to yourself, "Do I keep this or not? Was it mine to begin with or someone else's?" You get to choose.

We forget that we're the sole proprietors of us, that we get to choose whether we want to continue living with these thoughts, feelings, and beliefs. If not, then we get to rid ourselves of things that don't serve our greater good.

Remember—this is your life, not your friends', not your family's, and not society's. When you become more in tune with your higher self, you will see what fits and what doesn't— and you get to choose. You get to pick whatever it is that you want in your life.

Are you scared? Sure, it may feel scary. Try examining that feeling; you might realize that it's excitement instead of fear. In my own experience, whenever I think I feel scared, I realize that the feeling is really excitement. And when there's excitement, I know that there's a breakthrough and that something much greater is right around the corner. So what do I do? I get *more* excited. I play, get silly and listen to God, my Source as Anne and the next step lights up.

> God is the breath of life, the heart of hearts, the Self. To find Him means to find one's Self.
>
> —Sri Anandamahi Ma

It's so easy, it's ridiculous. I realized that in the past, I'd wasted so much time with worry, doubt, or fear. If I had focused on energy that was positive, I would have seen the next step light up on my path a whole lot earlier. Do I regret this wasted time? Of course not, because if it wasn't for that part of my path, I wouldn't be where I am today: more empowered than before, more abundant, healthier, and richer in so many ways.

I'm at that age that paying attention to how I expend my energy throughout the day is first and foremost. By doing so, I choose to prolong or shorten my life. In realizing this, I don't want to waste it on negative energy, thoughts, people, or experiences. I choose positivity!

Can I really be positive all the time? Probably not, but it's my goal and my focus. When I do lapse—and I do—I use my toys to bring me back to my Source, my true self, and my happy place.

How long does it take to shift your focus to being positive? It depends upon where you are on your path and to the degree in which you live daily as it varies with everyone. Since it took me a subconscious and gradual slide down the rabbit hole, the climb back out was gradual as well. There was no magic elixir taken one moment and completely relieved and healed the next. It's very important to understand that this is a journey. If you're looking for a quick fix, you'll be discouraged when it doesn't happen right away or overnight. Relax. Breathe. Play and have fun. See what happens. Don't take my word for it; I'm simply sharing what I know has worked well for me and for those I've taught. Find what brings you joy and enjoy that.

By utilizing these toys—or I should say, playing with my toys—I can get back my happy feeling faster and find joy in the moment. You can too, unless you choose to stay where you are.

I used to post this saying in my house, and it's really sunk in.

No matter where you go, there you are. Unless you move, the place where you are is the place you will always be. Your choice.

-Confuscious, Ashleigh Brilliant and Anne Ross

Using the toys in this book and learning what's essential for you to be happy will create more opportunities and possibilities for being content and peaceful no matter what's going on outside of you. You'll be healthier, have more meaningful relationships, achieve abundance, and live a more purpose-filled life.

You have no control over anyone or anything other than yourself. How you respond to things in the present will determine what happens in your life. When you're in a state of bliss or happiness in the moment, you create incredible opportunities of limitless possibility by attracting the same. That's where true happiness, joy, peace, and inner bliss reside.

We have so many desires, and most of the time we never get exactly what we desire, we come close or not at all. Why? Because we are always wanting and in a desirous view or because we're focusing on what we're lacking and what we haven't achieved. Focusing on what we want while feeling joy and happiness will attract the same kind of energy, and we'll start achieving those desires. Like attracts like.

A good place to start is to assess exactly how you feel right now. Take a body scan of how you're feeling.

- ♦ Are you feeling pressure in your heart?
- ♦ Is your stomach tense?
- ♦ Do you have a backache or headache?

Take note without judgment; simply provide yourself with feedback. Tell yourself that everything is going to be okay and that you will be taken care of. Don't argue with yourself. Remember—no judgment. Breathe and relax. Find the feeling that gives you great joy.

Read each section that follows with a clear mind and heart. If you want a quick fix, it is not going to happen, and you will be frustrated. Relax and take your time. Look outside or go for a walk. As you read this book, you will find something that resonates with you. If you are willing to allow yourself time to try to develop new, healthy habits, you will see the long-term benefits in time.

Being aware is the first step in achieving your desires. You are meant to reach your desires, to have dreams, and to be happy and joy-filled. Take one step at a time. Remember when you were a small child learning to walk, you didn't walk across the room confidently the first time. You took a single step. Focus on taking one step at a time, and in time you will get there. Be easy on yourself, be easy on the process, and appreciate what is in your life now.

Most important, take care of yourself. Be selfish! If you don't take care of yourself first, then you can't take care of others to share the wonderful gifts that you have to offer. I learned this the hard way. I was always the good girl, the savior to others, and I made my needs come last. When I was growing up in our home, I would help my mom because I loved her and wanted to be with her, and, because it was expected. As I matured and moved on, I was still the go-to girl for anyone. Over the years, I realized that my energy became depleted, and more important, I did not enjoy life because I wasn't living *my* life. I was living the life others wanted or needed me to live so *they* could be happy. But I was not happy!

I had to completely change the way I lived my life. I did a lot of soul-searching and got help. At this point, I started anew and was reborn. As I gained knowledge and understanding, I found my voice. For me to be happy, I used the toys that are described in this book and created the life I desired—not anyone else's desires for me and of me. I addressed *my* desire for *my* life.

I know that sounds selfish, but as I stated above, you need to be selfish and take care of your needs first. You must understand that this type of selfishness is not ego-based. It is about taking care of your basic needs, feeding your mind, body, and soul with nourishments to not just survive but to thrive. The nourishments are what I refer to as toys, and just to name a few; breath work, meditation, positive and loving affirmations, healthy food, exercise, playing, and having fun. The toys in this book are meant to remind us of the children that we are and how important it is to be playful, be in touch with our source God, to live the life of our desires, be creative, and cocreate with God and others in collaborative, fun play. Whatever that particular play is for you, be sure you play. We all have special gifts, and when we add play and fun into the mix, life is exhilarating.

I know people in a wide variety of careers, including plumbing, painting, and accounting. I am truly amazed at how happy and fulfilled they are, doing what they do because they are happy with themselves. I also know people who are very successful based on what they believe society deems successful—but they are not very healthy or happy. It's a choice. You have choices every moment of every day. You get to choose your path.

When I married my husband, I knew that he was going to be an accountant and a CPA. On the other hand, I am very creative, love to sew one-of-a-kind quilts, and love to play with fabric and texture. I also love to be with people, and for some reason people who are in pain and need help come to me. That is why I became a certified spiritual life coach. When my husband asked me to help him in his business, I helped. I do not like accounting; to me, it is boring. I bridged the two, playing as director of wellness in his practice. We work, but we have fun in the mix of it all. Why? Why not? It breaks up the energy-zapping monotony of accounting, for me, and we lighten the seriousness of what accounting can be to others. I create the fun in our time together at the office.

For example, we made a video called "Happy CPAs," which can be seen on YouTube. We have tacky Christmas sweater parties. Leprechauns visited the office on St. Patrick's Day, making little messes and spreading chocolate coins everywhere. Our clients received small pots of coins, and they loved it and laughed! We are hearing more and more from our clients about how enjoyable and fun it is to come to our office.

When we are in our happy place doing the work that represents who we are, it lightens up the room, and the energy is higher. When this happens, it is much easier to find solutions and get results than when we do work that doesn't bring us joy. Our office flows much better because we can easily get back on track. Our clients have commented they actually look forward to coming in for their tax appointments. Who would typically like *that*?

This joyful and playful environment, in turn, helps others to feel less resistance, facilitating greater rapport, trust, and freedom through a healthy, collaborative relationship with the accountants. The environment fosters success for all, and people go out into their respective worlds better equipped to share love and compassion.

Being loving and compassionate while serving others with your gift is your true purpose. Serving others will give you joy, whether this service comes in the form of family relationships, volunteer work, or your chosen career or purpose.

As you progress through this book, I encourage you to take notes; write in the margins, highlight words that have particular meaning to you, and color outside the box. Be joy-filled, be happy, and be free!

Chapter 4

Belief System

I do not fix my problems. I fix my thinking.
The problems fix themselves.

—Louise Hay

Our belief systems are individually created by us through our thoughts and the interpretations of those thoughts. We are born perfect, whole, and complete. It is through our own personal life paths and experiences that we create our belief systems.

We create thoughts from an unconscious viewpoint. We become aware or conscious of a thought, and if a thought gains momentum, it becomes a belief. For each belief—and we can have many—we choose in the moment to keep or discard the belief. If we choose to validate and keep a belief, each subsequently related experience will provide more data, proof, and results that will enlarge the belief (good or bad) and keep it perpetuating. This belief gains more momentum and becomes bigger and more concrete within our cellular structure.

As mentioned earlier, I had some experiences very early in my life that did not empower me in strong, positive beliefs. From those experiences:

- ◆ I created a belief system that in turn created an emotion.
- ◆ I placed meaning onto that emotion, which led me to behave in a certain way, negatively influencing the results.
- ◆ I kept arriving at undesirable results because I had cemented into my being a certain behavior *based on beliefs I continued to choose to anchor.*

It wasn't until I was much older, implemented meditation, conducted extensive research, and took advantage of psychoanalysis and therapy that I finally learned *I had to change the way I looked at my beliefs.*

When you change the way you look at things,
the things you look at change.

—Dr. Wayne Dyer

I realized that *I was not my beliefs.*

When I began playing with my toys, my life changed for the better, and in turn, these changes positively impacted the people around me through the energy shift that occurred within me. Changing my beliefs changed my life.

It is important to know that you have created beliefs because they worked for you in the past to survive. But these beliefs *may* have no useful purposes any longer. Or perhaps your beliefs were copied or mirrored from an authoritative or influential person—a parent, neighbor, relative, pastor, teacher, school administrator, or other person in the community. If you mirrored beliefs from someone you felt had influence or power over you, you may have done so because you felt that "in order to survive," you had to acquiesce to that person's influential power. That energy is negative energy because it probably doesn't feel good. I had those same feelings, and they didn't feel good. I didn't have the toys to play with and to help me reject those feelings. I didn't have the confidence to discard them or walk away. At times, it seemed like a struggle just to survive.

Think about an experience for which your perception of the experience previously caused you some level of pain. Or perhaps you have had an experience in which you felt that a person has wronged you, and you feel some level of angst when you think of that person. You internalized and personalized that experience, and then each subsequent thought or experience with or without that person has triggered more undesirable feelings and behaviors. Those in turn add more data to your belief system, and it becomes a vicious cycle. The negative feelings and behaviors may have increased. At times, it seems as if it has consumed your life. Has this feeling and belief affected how you live your life?

When you become more aware and realize that you may have uncomfortable feelings and behaviors, you have achieved success. I know, you are thinking, "Is she nuts?" No! When we become *aware* of our truths, negative or positive, we have taken a big step toward healing. The act of *becoming aware* is a success. It may seem daunting and scary, and I agree wholeheartedly, but I wouldn't be where I am today if I had not slowed my life almost to a standstill, pondered, assessed what I was doing, and took the first step toward healing.

First, I called my closest friends, who had sought professional help to deal with life experiences, and I asked for referrals. Second, I found outside help. I started making calls and inquiring about services. Being my own advocate for healing was my driving force. I have not stopped since. I've moved on from the initial expert therapies and have other people in my life that I consult on a regular basis to guide, support, and assist me on my journey. To these friends, I am eternally grateful because I could not have done it without them. I am so blessed to continue to have them in my life.

Finding books, seminars, and spiritual places is my mothership. I use these resources all the time. They give me great joy and peace of mind. I am a spiritual warrior, ferociously curious and very passionate about spreading my passion to anyone who is curious or seeking help. I love what I do, and I do what I love. Keeping it simple helps. Yes, I do still feel overwhelmed at times. When this happens, I play with my toys, utilize deep breathing, find a quiet place, go outside, or meditate. Negative and painful experiences in my life have been my greatest teachers, and for those experiences I am also very grateful. I did not feel or think this way for a long time.

My philosophy is that each of us has the ability to find our truth and support that truth, whatever it is, with positive and healing modalities as long as it is for the greater good of all.

With that said, sometimes to support the greater good, it is best to temporarily step away. If you continue to have bad feelings after stepping away, distance yourself, take a sabbatical from this person, seek coaching, and take a timeout to heal within. During this pause, ask yourself, "What if the person's actions or statements had nothing to do with me?"

Just as your perceptions of the original experience were based upon how you felt in the moment and the sum total of your current summary of experiences, the person who "wronged" you may have been acting out of his or her own fear-based perception of the experience. It is important to consider the following:

- Your fear is *your* fear.

- The offender's responses or actions may have been reasonable for that person based upon where he or she was at that time and place. Continuing to blame and shame this person based on past experiences will not allow you to move forward—it will only perpetuate your belief that he or she was wrong, creating a vicious cycle.

- Examine your belief regarding the person who you felt wronged you. Consider the possibility that *you* had nothing to do with the person's actions. This bears repeating, so please pause and ponder this: consider the possibility that *you* had nothing to do with the person's actions.

- To grow spiritually and gain a healthy perspective, it is important to look upon the person and those originating incidents with empathy, understanding, and compassion for what circumstances might have led to that person's actions. Can you do this without personalizing and internalizing the feelings that make you feel like a victim?

- If you still insist that this person has wronged you, ask yourself this question: "How do I know this is true?" Ask this question in front of a mirror. Look into your eyes and examine the feeling that comes up for you.

Test yourself. Think of the person and pay close attention to your immediate gut feelings. How do you feel? Do you have any discomfort? Keep working on this process periodically. When you can think of the person for more than a few minutes without having uncomfortable feelings, you will be well on your way to recovery and living a joy-filled life. The true test is the test itself. Breathing and finding your place of joy will be your reward.

The key is to test yourself when you are feeling happy because you are already in a good place. Testing yourself when you are in a not-so-good place will yield a negative result—what some professionals refer to as a double negative. You definitely don't want that. Be easy with yourself.

Go play and have fun. In time, the pain and effort of relating to this person, or anyone who creates a negative trigger or fear, will diminish.

By being your own advocate and doing the inner work, to find your inner peace, will the negativity and fears diminish. You have to do your own inner work.

What if, in your perception, the person never changes? Most likely, the person involved in the original creation of your negative belief system said or did something and moved on from it. But what if you are in a relationship with someone who contributed to a negative belief system and that person *continues* to engage in statements and actions that strain your relationship by creating bad feelings and/or triggering defensive behaviors? You may need to consider cutting the cord in that particular relationship. Cutting the cord is a figurative term used to describe cutting the umbilical cord between a parent and child, but it is also often used to describe cutting a tie or link in any familial or nonbiological relationship. Any of these relationships might need a severing for you to heal. This process can be done through visualization or hypnosis. If you are new to this type of healing, it is best to connect with someone (such as a life coach or therapist) so that you properly understand and possibly undergo treatment if needed.

Whether you cut the cord or distance yourself from this person, there may be times when you experience these same feelings again. As you meet other people who remind you of past negative experiences, the interactions will trigger negative reactions until you heal from within through reevaluation or (when necessary) permanent distancing. Take the time to heal. Love yourself. Find what makes you happy, keep adding to that feeling, surround yourself with people who provide you with support and who cherish you for who you are, and surround yourself with places and things that bring you comfort and joy. You cannot serve yourself or anyone else if you are not coming from a place of unconditional love, compassion, and joy. Be selfish. Self-care is essential to your vitality. Play and have fun.

Consider another aspect to this type of relationship: *you* might be a trigger for this person. For some known or unknown reason, when you are present in this person's life, you cause him or her to behave in a negative manner. The person may not even be aware of this. Your energy triggers a discomfort and subsequent negativity.

I have had experiences throughout my life in which individuals behaved negatively, or I sensed something that was not congruent between us. At first I would try very hard to turn them around by changing myself and my behavior. I was concerned with the fact that they "just didn't get me," and I wanted to fix that. The problem with that is that I was trying once again to be someone I was not in order for others to be happy about themselves. I eventually learned that it was okay for them to not get me, agree with me, or like me.

One of the biggest breakthroughs for me, as it is for many people in similar situations, was to understand that everyone is fighting some kind of battle to some degree. When I am around people who react in a negative manner, I try to stand in their shoes. Although I do not need to know the specifics of their pain and suffering, I can have compassion and send them love and healing.

You must understand that people have to heal themselves. Whenever people act negatively toward you, their behaviors are based out of their own self-induced fears. When people demonstrate behaviors around me that are not neutral or happy, I know that I am not the problem; the problem stems from their own suffering. Something about our interactions cause them to consciously or subconsciously go back in time.

Our interactions are triggers, and the negative behaviors can be triggered by me or someone else at any given moment. People create behavioral momentum with certain beliefs, and when the beliefs are triggered, they automatically go to a certain place. This momentum is so quick sometimes those behaviors can change like night and day in a matter of nanoseconds. The reason for this is because the beliefs are embedded within their cellular structure based upon repeated performances throughout their lives. When people don't realize this, they keep playing the same record over and over again. Even if they consciously know they behave this way, they believe they can change the outcome by changing their behavior. This will not happen because they don't realize it is their belief system that needs changing, or they aren't aware of the particular belief that needs changing.

We all have events and experiences in our lives that cause us to act or react in a manner that might not be for our best interests. We may feel odd, or our energy sinks a little. At these events or experiences, we go back to a specific age in which our emotional needs were not met. We then behave based upon survival skills that we created long ago and that helped us get through whatever it was we were trying to survive.

As we grow up, we are continually presented with experiences that test our belief systems. These pop quizzes, midterms, and final exams, if you will, test us to see if we're still operating with unlearned emotional maturity. This maturity is unlearned because we have not learned the lesson and have not achieved awareness, understanding, and success of that particular emotional age. As we learn life's lessons, our emotional maturity enables us to deal more effectively with emotional triggers.

Taking a few deep breaths and having compassion for ourselves and the other person is empowering. When we come from a place of peace and compassion, we begin to see that the other is in pain. Rather than be defensive or negative in response, we can love them as they are in that moment. When in a battle of words, it is most helpful to stop, breathe, and walk away. That action will break the momentum and will give both of you time.

There are people I have had to let go of and cut the cord, and it's all good. I send them love and love them from afar. That is what works for me; it may not work for them, but that is not my initial concern. I used to live my life to please others first, and that didn't work for me. It was not in my best interest. I used the toys here in this book, used my voice and stood up for myself while loving them.

When I realized that there was no further need to continue in the relationship, I lovingly cut the cord. That is very important: even if the other person doesn't understand and continues to make contact with you, you do not have to respond. You can remove someone from your daily interactions. I recommend doing this slowly, and eventually they may decrease their contact, totally stop making contact with you, or change.

Find your happy place. Be loving and compassionate toward yourself, and in time this will come back to you tenfold. It might not come back to you from the people with whom you've had negative experiences, but it *will* come back to you.

There is a saying: "People come into your life for a reason, a season, or a lifetime." This rings true for everyone in your life, no matter if people are blood related or lifelong friends. Go with your flow and be happy.

Do you need assistance on this path? You can change the way you look at your own beliefs by spending time getting reacquainted with your true authentic self through compassion and love. Life coaches are neutral, understanding, and accepting. They will assist you in tracing your beliefs back to an earlier age by listening to you and understanding where you are right now. They will then develop a specialized treatment for you, incorporating their own tools or possibly utilizing the toys I use every day, such as guidance, counseling, breath work, meditation, and hypnosis or use their own modalities they feel will be the best for you.

If led into hypnosis, a good life coach will create a *safe* environment for you; that is first and foremost. They will take you back to the earliest time possible, continuing to instill trust, safety, and love. The safe environment will enable you to go to the place where you experienced a fear, which created the belief. With that in mind, know that everything is going to be okay because when guided back to that experience, you will be watching from above, not physically experiencing the event again. It is similar to watching your life on TV: you will be safe and will feel a sense of trust and security.

Prior to the hypnosis, coaches will build a trusting relationship with you. They care very much about how you will be able to handle sensitive situations. You may have feelings and insights that have been repressed and that you will experience for the first time, and it's the life coach who is sensitive to your well-being with regard to your ability to handle what you will see or sense during coaching sessions.

Throughout the hypnosis process, a coach will be very astute to what you are going through physically and emotionally. After a process, you and your coach will spend time to evaluate the hypnosis process and discuss your experience.

The hypnosis experience will enable you to release something that has been held within, possibly for a very long time. It is refreshing because you've released it, although it may not seem refreshing at first. Most individuals already understand the connections between their thoughts, beliefs, actions, and reactions to events; this is why they seek counsel and guidance. They are usually having a difficult time in their life, are experiencing physical or emotional instability, and are seeking answers and relief in order to more fully understand the link and do the work necessary to heal.

Life coaches are very interested in your growth and want to work with you in advancing your awakening into your true, authentic self. It is life-transforming for your greater good.

Chapter 5

Energy

What you think about activates a vibration within you. Think abundantly. Energy follows intention.

—Law of Attraction

Although I address this topic here, I feel it is the most important aspect of all of the teachings. However, I wanted to give you a few things to ponder first to get a good grasp of my teachings. I believe that it is important to understand energy, also called vibration, and become more aware of it in every moment; it will change your life exponentially for the better, for the greater good. Know this:

Everything is energy. Energy is in everything.

Energy is in everything that we see, hear, taste, and sense. Energy is in us and is our skin, clothing, furniture, and the air that we breathe. Our bodies are constantly producing energy, and it is regulated by many things such as the heart. Whether it is mitochondria or the cells that keep producing upon themselves, energy runs the heart.

What is this energy that runs the heart is in the air that we breathe, and is in our clothing and furniture? Where does this energy come from? I am not a scientist or a doctor, but what I do know is that the source that gives me the energy to keep me alive is God. What runs this source of energy? That is a marvelous question.

In Polynesian and Melanesian cultures, they use the term *Mana* to describe an extraordinary power or force residing in a person or an object, sort of spiritual electricity that charges anyone who touches it. Carl Jung defines the term as "the unconscious influence of one being on another."

For me, it is being in alignment with my source, God. When I'm feeling joy-filled and am allowing this energy of spirit to flow through me and to others, it is amazing, and gifts and miracles appear. Without uttering a word, I am able to see God in everything and everyone, and whatever I'm seeking is put right in front of me for the joy of receiving. When this happens, it ignites my being, and I become more energized so I can keep shining brightly and giving it to those around me.

Think back to chapter 3. Do you remember when I asked you to sit for a moment and remember being a happy child, and I asked you what it felt like? It is that feeling that I want you to grab on to and practice, because this feeling is the key to happiness. How you feel creates how your life is, how it is going to be, and what you are attracting to yourself.

Once you learn to sense energy, you'll be more able to assess your own feelings, others, and situations. More important, you will improve your ability to connect with God and expand upon your experience with this amazing source. I have expanded my knowledge about the teachings of God, Yahweh, and Jesus Christ, Buddha, Inanna and other names for our source. The more I know, the more I realize how much more there is to know. When I continue to expand my awareness, I remove any limitations I might have in understanding others and their beliefs; this allows me to more openly examine experiences, ask questions, and receive answers in order to come into alignment with God and my authentic self. I have found this to be a simple, fun, and wonderful experience of enlightenment. I'm more peaceful, happy, and content. It is as though a weight has been lifted, and I have a clarified purpose and am able to experience more successful relationships and improved health and abundance.

Energy functions best when it's in balance. You can clear your mind, optimize your wellness, become more intuitive, have insight to your gifts, pursue your purpose, and be happier.

Let's play a game. Consider one aspect of energy: fear. Fear can manifest itself as anger, quiet anger, depression, bullying, anxiety, doubt, resisting, sarcasm, stress, control, greed, fatigue, bossiness, passive-aggressive behavior, a know-it-all attitude, and more. Close your eyes and think of an incident that triggered fear or one of these emotions for you. As you recall that experience, take a body scan. How do you feel, and *where* are you feeling it? Starting with your head, take note of any tension, pain, pressure, or other *negative* energy. Stay with that energy for a few minutes; focus on the uncomfortable sensation. Try to relax and breathe. You may notice that the feeling fades away, or not. Continue this body scan from head to toe. By learning to relieve the feeling of fear as a symptom, you can reduce or eliminate the negative manifestations. You create; manifest all of your feelings. No one else does that for you. Someone or something may trigger these feelings within you, but you are ultimately responsible for creating all of your thoughts, feelings, and experiences.

Breathe and breathe again, find your happy place, and let's continue the game.

Love is another aspect of energy. Love is the truth, and the truth always prevails. Always! Love appears as childlike joy, happiness, genius, creativity, exuberance, excitement, resourceful, silliness, intelligence, playfulness, contentment, peace, calm, and an openness to receive anything, even in the face of intense anger or rage. Coming from a place of unconditional love allows the calm mind and heart to handle anything in any situation no matter how intense the negativity is that is happening outside of us. Close your eyes and think of an experience that evokes feelings of love. Take a body scan. Where do you feel love? How do you feel when you recall this experience? Do you notice how relaxed and at peace you feel? Was this part of the game easier than when I asked you to experience fear? Sit with this for a while, and ponder how you were able to manifest both types of emotions and feelings. Take an assessment of the polar opposite of these thoughts and feelings. You may want to start journaling what your body is sensing when you have this or any other emotional experience.

Love is the feeling that is instrumental in a happy life—your life. This is how you will want to feel most of the time. With practice, you will feel the energy of love more often. Can you imagine for a moment what your life will look like by playing with energy, feeling love, being able to see yourself to allow the feeling of love and happiness at any moment during a life experience? Oh, it is so much fun!

God, thank you for shining your light upon me and reminding me of who I truly am: a child of God who can play full out, have fun, be happy, and be in love with myself, other humans and animals, nature, and the cosmos. Wow! I am so grateful for these experiences and the ability to see and know my truth. I know that I can have all my desires. I am so very grateful. Thank you.

The great masters of enlightenment, the self-realization of God are in a state of bliss and joyous consciousness. The polar opposite is fear and chaos. In the diagram below, the continuum of chaos to joyous consciousness is represented as a funnel. The upper part—the area that is bliss, joyous consciousness, and love—is larger, wider. You can imagine being able to receive more in that state than you can when you are functioning in chaos, the lower part of the funnel, which looks pinched off, shut down, and easy to clog up.

Omega
Chart

700+	Enlightenment	Ultimate Consciousness
600	Peace	
540	Joy	
500	Love	
400	Reason	Expanded
350	Acceptance	
310	Willingness	
250	Neutrality	
200	Courage	
175	Pride	
150	Anger	
125	Desire	
100	Fear	Contracted
75	Grief	
50	Apathy	
30	Guilt	
20	Shame	

If something gets stuck, you will not be able to get through it because it is so small. Have you ever felt stuck or clogged up with stuff, like you were wading through a mild river of misery? I have, and it does not feel so great. What was worse, I couldn't get myself unstuck; it slowed me down, and I became fatigued. If you're tired of being stuck, the answer is to use the toys and play. You and only you can unclog yourself. What are you waiting for?

Several times in my life I have felt like I was waiting for someone, something, the answer, or a tool to get me out of it. I had been given the next step, but I wasn't willing to see it because I was so caught up in the hamster wheel of misery, running, spinning, and getting more tired. I knew that who I was at my most stuck was not my truth. How did I know this? Because I became aware. I started disassociating from myself. When I did that, I would watch myself and know that I knew better, because I had experienced fun, happiness, and playfulness before. I had a guidepost, and remember—I had that sense, that *voice*, speak to me as a young child out in nature that everything was going to be okay and that I would be taken care of.

I internally asked for help. Teachers would appear, whether physically or in a book on the subject matter I was researching. The first book that spoke to me was Louise Hay's *You Can Heal Your Life* in 1987. I still have that book; I refer to it, use it, and apply the principles to this day. My library has grown exponentially. When I started on this path, I converted from pleasure reading to self-help, healing, and enlightenment and I incorporated yoga and meditation. Then the class work began—literally. That was when I really looked into delving deeper on an academic basis. I ventured to the California

Institute of Integral Studies in San Francisco and was blown away by their Eastern teachings and influences.

Do you see a pattern taking place? I was stopped, stuck. I found one thing that started my path. Then another, and then another. I gained momentum—slowly at first, but momentum nonetheless and in the right direction. I just as easily could have gone the other direction, and Lord knows where I would be today.

At my lowest point, a friend advised me to take an antidepressant to help my depressed feeling. Why on earth would I do that? If I created the feeling, the thoughts that got me there, then nothing in the world could help me but me! I had to do the work that I am so passionate about and want to share and shout to the world about. Why? Because it gives me pure joy and happiness when I am doing my thing. I had to experience the dark side so I could figure out how to get to the light, on my own. No one else was going to do the inner work for me, and pharmaceutical or other placebo, was going to do it either.

I believe that 90 percent of your inspiration, direction, and motivation come from listening to your heart and gut. You really only need your mind or brain for 10 percent of your daily needs and the choices you make, such as balancing your checkbook or knowing when to put gas in your car. Listen to your gut where intuition resides. Feel what is going on inside, and understand that heart-centered choices will always direct you on your path—the right path. This is your connection to God.

Find the happiness within. Tap into your childlike outlook. Start seeing and playing with energy. See what happens. Remember that this is for the greater good of all. Also, when you start focusing on bettering yourself, finding your happy place, and sometimes even being a little selfish, then your life will be so much healthier and more abundant, fun, and happy.

Let's play one more energy game. Go to a park, zoo, or aquarium. Watch young children playing, investigating, finding, and seeing something for the first time. Watch how they express themselves so easily and freely. Now, be like that, even if you think or feel like you will be embarrassed.

My most fun and happiest times are when I act childlike in public. I take selfies with my family and friends. People come up and ask if they can take my picture. I smile and thank them and tell them that I love to do selfies. They smile, and that is a gift. Wow! What is even more fun is posting my selfies on Facebook and seeing the comments and likes. No, I am not out *for* the response, but I enjoy the responses I get when I do this; it serves no other purpose than pure joy. When I am in this state of happy, blissful being, I am helping others to lighten up, shine, and hopefully, maybe help someone snap out of being in a bad mood. How do I know this? I can feel it. The energy in a room or outside changes, and I can usually see it in their faces and smiles; and fewer wrinkles. If you don't believe me, try it. You just might like it. Who knows maybe I'll see your selfie and post a happy comment.

I know you might be asking yourself, "Why should I?" All I have to say is, "Why not?"

Now, go get your energy on!

Chapter 6

Breathing

You don't always need a plan. Sometimes you
just need to breathe, trust, let go, and see what
happens.

—Mandy Hale

Being conscious of your breath and learning different breathing
techniques can assist you in creating happiness, peace, and
clarity, as well as helping you feel more energized. The lack
of mindful breathing is considered to be the greatest barrier
to attaining a deep state of meditation. By focusing on your
breath, you can achieve a deep calmness.

The three types of breathing are clavicular, intercostal, and
deep abdominal breathing.

♦ Clavicular breathing is very shallow and is achieved by
raising the shoulders and collarbone while contracting
the abdomen. Although maximum effort is made, the
body only receives a minimum amount of air. This is
the least efficient type of breathing: air fills only the
upper third of the lungs.

♦ Intercostal breathing, the second type of incomplete breathing, involves raising the clavicle, shoulders, and torso and expanding the chest wall and ribs. Again, air fills only the upper third of the lungs.

♦ Deep abdominal breathing, or diaphragmatic breathing, uses the diaphragm to achieve the most efficient breathing, bringing air to the lowest and largest part of the lungs. Breathing is slow and deep.

Even diaphragmatic breathing isn't "complete." A full yogic breath combines all three breathing types, beginning with the abdomen and continuing the inhalation through the intercostal and clavicular areas.

Below are several breathing techniques that will assist you. The key is awareness and practice.

Diaphragmatic Breathing. To breathe properly, one should begin with the diaphragm, the membrane that separates the lungs from the visceral cavity. The diaphragm works with a downward movement that causes the lungs to expand, creating a lower air pressure within the lungs than outside the body. Thus, air is drawn into the lungs. The downward movement of the diaphragm forces the stomach outward. If your stomach does not expand as you inhale, you are not breathing diaphragmatically.

The following is the best way to learn diaphragmatic breathing. Wear loose clothing and lie on your back. Place a hand on the upper abdomen, where the diaphragm is located. Breathe in and out slowly. The abdomen should expand outward as you inhale and contract as you exhale. Try to get the feeling of this motion. Breathe in slowly and expand the abdomen, then the rib cage, and finally the upper portion of the lungs. Then breathe out in the same manner, letting the abdomen cave in as much as you can as you slowly exhale. This is the complete yogic breath. This is how you breathe when you are in a deep sleep, when the body is completely relaxed. Diaphragmatic breathing becomes natural and effortless.

When used correctly—expanding the diaphragm, the floating ribs, and the lungs to include the upper part of your chest—you will fill your whole body with energy. By practicing this method over time, you will begin seeing and feeling changes in your life for the better. You will realize that you are calmer during experiences that previously may have caused you to tense up. Your thoughts will be more at peace, and in turn, your reactions or nonreactions in various situations will be neutral or joyful, as well as void of stress, shallow breathing, and negative thinking.

Sit in a comfortable chair upright, with your palms up on your lap. Close your eyes. Take a deep breath, fill your lungs, and push your diaphragm out as far as you can. Keep expanding your lungs, chest, and shoulders, lifting upward as much as you can to the count of six. (As you advance, you can achieve a count of up to twelve.) Hold while repeating, "Om Shanti Om." Then release to the same count of six. Do this three times and then resume your regular breathing pattern. This is a great routine prior to meditation.

Hong–Sau Breath. In Hindu, Hong-Sau translates to "I am." Take a deep diaphragmatic breath for a count of six while saying "Hong" ("I"). Hold for a count of three and release your breath for a count of six while saying "Sau" ("am"). Continue this pattern, saying the mantra "Hong Sau" in a more regular breathing pattern. This great breathing technique can be used continuously throughout meditation.

Japa Breath. This is a more advanced breathing tool. You will need to be very mindful of your throat because you control the breath by constricting your windpipe as you breathe in and out. Similar to the technique used by musicians who play the oboe and flute, you will constrict your throat and slowly take in a deep diaphragmatic breath. Hold for a count of three and then exhale in the same, very controlled manner. It is as if you are being very conscious of every molecule of air coming in and out. This is a great technique to use if you have an anxious stomach.

Controlled diaphragmatic breathing is a link to connecting to the Source. When I inhale and exhale, I feel as if God is breathing life into me, creating more vibrant and healthy cells, which in turn vitalize and energize every part of my mind, body, and soul.

You can use the Japa breathing technique with Japa Mala beads, a string of 108 Hindu prayer beads with a large 109th Guru bead (also known as the Meru, Bindu, or Sumaru bead). It is used for keeping count during mantra meditations. There are also wrist malas made of twenty-seven beads. Here's how to use Mala beads during meditation:

1. Follow the breathing tips above and the tips in chapter 7 for preparing for meditation.
2. Decide the intention of your meditation and select a mantra or affirmation.
3. Hang the large Guru bead on your middle or ring finger of your right hand. Extend your index finger (representing ego), because it should not touch the mala. The large bead should not be touched or counted; it is used as a starting and ending point.
4. Touch the first bead after the Guru bead. Begin reciting your mantra or affirmation. Use your thumb to push

the bead away from you and continue your mantra or affirmation with the next bead.

5. Continue until you have repeated your mantra for all beads. If you are using a 27-bead wrist mala, cycle through the beads four times for a total of 108 repetitions.

6. In Hindu tradition, if more than one mala of repetitions is to be done, change directions when you reach the Guru bead rather than cross it.

Chapter 7

Meditation

Sometimes your only transportation is a leap
of faith.

—Margaret Shepherd

I love to meditate. With our busy world swirling around at
lightning speed, meditation allows us to go to the empty space
where we can be the calm in the eye of the storm. Within this
place of peace, meditation affords us the opportunity to get
back to our center, be with God, and most important open
our minds to receive downloads and answers to our questions,
providing us with clarity and energy.

In the beginning your thoughts will run rampant. This
is natural. You have been running the same sixty thousand
thoughts per day, so it will take some time to quiet the mind.
If you find your mind wandering as you prepare to meditate,
try the following technique. It has worked for me, but you
may want to come up with your own. Tell your mind, "I
am thinking," or, "Release." Picture a thought bubble and
visualize tapping it with a feather so that the bubble disappears.
The rampant, racing thoughts will decrease over time, and as
you devote more time to meditation, you will notice a change

in your day-to-day life: you will be more at peace, feel calmer, and think more clearly.

There are many ways to meditate, but the most important thing is to have a quiet place to open your mind. Some people use meditation pillows or boards to sit upon; these are positioned on the floor in a peaceful place, void of noise and commotion. If you don't have access to these, do the best you can with what is available to you.

Sit comfortably with legs crossed in the lotus position, with your palms placed upward on your knees and your back straight. If sitting in the lotus position on the floor is not comfortable for you, sit in a chair with your palms and back the same as for sitting on the floor. Close your eyes. Utilizing one of the breathing methods mentioned in chapter 6, become centered with your breathing; the type of breathing you need to relax may vary from situation to situation. Start by taking three deep diaphragmatic breaths and then get into your regular breathing. Advance to Hong-Sau Breath or Japa Breath until you can relax.

Once you have learned to control your breathing, you can pose a question prior to meditating. If the answer is neutral or positive and comes from your gut or heart, you know you are in touch with your Spirit. *Do not attempt to answer the question yourself, or to question the answers you receive.* When you start to question the answers, then you know your mind or ego is questioning your God. Quiet the mind. At first it will seem too quick or too easy, but that is exactly what it is: easy.

For example, after I have done my three deep breaths and then breathed in a regulated pattern, I will ask specific questions. This allows my quiet mind to receive the messages that I need to hear. One of the best sequence of questions I like to ask is as follows:

- Where do you want me to go?
- What do you want me to do?
- What do you want me to say, and to whom?

I don't always get an immediate response. When this happens, I complete my meditation and then slowly and calmly start my day. The answer sometimes becomes clear when I am out and about during my day. Something will come up that directs me to the next step on my path. I may pick up information from someone or something I am engaging with that resonates with me. It could be a store clerk, a billboard sign, or a song on the radio. Sometimes the message I receive has nothing to do with my meditation question, but it is clearly the answer I need. This usually leads me to something, and then something else after that. Try to approach asking your questions with no judgment. Don't question the answers; simply ask and receive the responses. Be patient.

Alice: How long is forever?
White Rabbit: Sometimes only for one second.

—Lewis Carroll

I know you are getting antsy for the answer to "How long do I have to meditate?" If it's easier for you to have a defined goal, start with fifteen minutes, just so you start and keep it going. Even five minutes of closing your eyes and being conscious of your breathing is a good start. When I first started meditating, I would try to do it until I could quiet my mind enough to know that I could do it. If you are seeking enlightenment, meditation is key. I have been meditating for more than fifteen years, and I continue to see the benefits. It's another game for me to play with that assists me on my path of expanding my self-realization. My recommendation is to simply start and keep meditating. You will see tremendous benefits, including a positive impact on your health, relationships, and purpose.

During the day, practice five or more minutes of meditation. Look outside, go outside, or sit at your desk. Close your eyes and quiet your mind. In the long run, this will help you tremendously. Give yourself time and be patient with the process. The whole purpose of meditation is to become calm and peaceful. No matter what is going on around you or what is happening in your life, you can be your true, authentic, joy-filled self and live happier in the present moment. Ask the questions, listen, be still, breathe, be patient, and keep at it!

You might also find benefit in using meditation CDs. In the back of the book, you will find an appendix listing suggested reading materials and meditation CDs. Find one that you like and change it up over time, if needed. When I started meditating, I did not use anything except patience while focusing on my breathing. Everyone is different; choose what works best for you.

Chapter 8

Affirmations

I am the light of the World.

—Jesus, John 8:12

An affirmation is something that does just what its name sounds like: it is a statement that affirms something. Use affirmations to change your state, to direct your attention toward what you know to be your authentic self. Affirming is a way to remind yourself of what you know to be your truth and to continue on your path of expansion-building that you truly desire. Your truth is a compassionate, loving, creative, joy-filled, playful, and expansive energy/being.

Sometimes we find ourselves on the hamster wheel of fear. We have allowed something or someone to cause our egos to return to a place that is not in accordance with who we truly are. By affirming something, we are allowing all that does not serve our greater good to slip away, to free us to be our truth. Examples of positive affirmations are as follows:

- ♦ I am calm.
- ♦ I am peace.
- ♦ I am love.

- I am forgiveness.
- Joy and energy descend upon me.
- I am healthy.
- Every cell and system in my body is running at its perfect state of optimum health.
- I am achieving all of my wildest dreams all for the greater good.
- I am surrounded by loving and supportive people.
- I live in a healthy, happy home.
- I am on my true path and find each step easily.

The phrases are useful any time you feel the need to affirm something. There are days when I find myself off track, and I use these affirmations to remind me of my truth. As you progress with breathing and meditation, adding affirmations will increase the happy momentum. It is one more toy to keep you focused and on track. You might need affirmations in the morning to affirm how you want your day to go. You might find that you want more happy energy in the morning to achieve your desire for a more positive day. You can use affirmations at night to set intentions for sleeping well and to wake up on the right or as I like to call it the happy side of the bed.

There was a period in my life when I realized I was waking up on the wrong side of the bed. Upon awakening every day I made these affirmations. "I love me. I am very grateful for who I am and where I am in my life. I feel the joy of who I truly am every day." It was a bit of a challenge at first, but over time I eventually found I was waking up happy and at peace. Then the most wonderful thing occurred: I *was* happy without having to say the affirmations. I awoke happy without an effort; I felt happy and light. My being felt the peace, calm, and happiness without actually needing to say the words. Sometimes I cement affirmations by saying them three times while pumping my fist and saying, "Yes, yes, yes!"

As with breathing, meditation, or any new toy, using affirmations will take time. If you are considering starting this with the contingency that if you don't see any results after the first week, then out the window it goes, you are setting yourself up for sabotage by not allowing it to come to its full potential.

Be easy about yourself and about implementing all new toys, but be persistent! Even in the most challenging of times, persistence will pay off in time. It is like planting a seed and expecting a plant to be fully grown the next day: it is not going to happen. But by allowing it to take root while providing it with fertilizer, water, and patience, it will eventually flourish, blossom, and show its true beautiful self.

Keep in mind that if you have been living a life of habitually being a certain way or saying certain things that were not for the greater good for yourself or others, it will take time to reprogram your mind, body, and emotional being. This process is called neurolinguistic deprogramming to reprogram. You are deprogramming old beliefs, habits, and routines so you can rebuild and reprogram to a healthier you. It is similar to having an old computer that is slow and not functioning like it used to, and you take it to the computer shop for repair. What used to work sometimes needs to be repaired, reprogrammed, or receive a complete overhaul. Learning how to use a new program or computer takes time and patience. Be the same way with yourself as you might be with your computer.

Self-effort, focus, courage, and persistence is what creates consistency. This consistency will increase the momentum, and in turn, the continual momentum will help you achieve your desires. It will become your way of being.

Chapter 9

Intention

Happiness is when what you think, what you
say, and what you do are in harmony.

—Mahatma Gandhi

Stating an intention before a meeting, conversation, day,
or event will create an even more powerful and engaging
experience. Stating an intention is exactly what it sounds like:
you state the desired intention for something in which you are
about to engage. *Webster's Dictionary* defines intention as "an
act or instance of determining mentally upon some action or
result." When you affirm your intention, your focus will be
on what you actually see happening versus what you hope to
accomplish (see chapter 11, "Goal Setting"). Wishing, hoping,
and dreaming are great, and many people do it—but they stop
there. These wishes, hopes, and dreams await you *until you apply
the direct intention* to create the momentum to achieve them.

Here's an example of an intention: "I intend to be inspiring
in my presentation so clients will feel motivated to use the tools
and strategies I prescribe." Include as part of your intention,
"I intend for the experience to be for the greater good of all."
Setting the attention on intention creates focus and specifics.

Adding this intention will free you from going astray, having distractions, and developing attachment to a specific outcome. It's almost as if you are affirming a specific intention out to the universe, freely and with joy.

When you feel and say your intention, there is no doubt that your energy transcends to others. When you are in this state of heightened energy, light, purpose, and happiness, it empowers others and gives them permission to be in the same state. Being focused on your happiness transcends everything and everyone.

My ability to transcend occurred at the 2014 CPAmerica Conference. I had only spoken in front of an audience once previously, and that was a small audience. I prepared myself this time with affirming my intention of being energetically happy and passionate about my topic, and of being an inspiration. After my presentation, I was surrounded by a fully engaged, appreciative, and excited audience. I was not attached to hoping they would like me or my topic. I received the highest rating of all of the speakers at the weeklong conference. I was just me being me, passionate about my toys and how to use them, and I created a fun environment for others to play along with me. And, I had so much fun!

When we attach to a specific outcome, we will be disappointed because we set limitations on all parties involved, and in reality we have no control over anyone else. Without focusing on an intention, the result will frequently not be what we intended. We only have control over ourselves and how we respond to each moment.

Be happy, carefree, and in a state of joy and bliss all of the time. Approach experiences with love, even if it is an experience you believe you will not like. Enter situations with the intention to allow every person to be his or her true, authentic self. See the diversity and contrast in others, recognize that they were made to be the unique individuals they are, and understand that happiness comes in whatever shape or fashion we were all created.

Approaching situations with intentions will allow you to achieve a win–win for all. Why? Because when you focus on the intention and goodness in the collaboration, then the results will always be joy-filled.

Whatever happens is all good and is as it should be. Breathe and meditate for a few minutes, and then state your intention. Going into a situation with this perspective, and intention will generate a happy feeling, positive energy, as well as the opportunity to take relationships to the next level.

Stating the intention to everyone in the beginning of a meeting allows the people involved to know what is going to happen in the meeting and what the intended purpose and focus is. When and if the topic goes astray, you can remind others what the stated intention is and get back on track. You can always set another meeting to discuss the other topics, especially if you have limited time. You can always finish the intended topic and, if time allows, move on to the other topics brought up.

When you are in the experience with the stated intention at the forefront of your mind, you are more aware of being in the moment. By being in the moment and focusing on the greater good and a win–win, you are allowed to be more open to know what is needed. This is especially helpful in a meeting with a client or when you have to discuss something that might be sensitive for you and the other person. Intention allows you to be real, honest, and in integrity with your true self for the success, collaboration, and joy of participating in the intended desire.

This is especially helpful with clients. It gives the accountant the ability to keep an eye on time and get to the meat of the matter. If a client wants to discuss other matters, another meeting can be scheduled, and the current focus is kept intact.

Along with the intention of the meeting or conversation, it is also very important to express the offer that if for any reason you or the other party agrees to disagree, then all is good. Everyone needs to be able to be authentic and to present ideas. Find an agreeable, happy place for success and happiness for all, even if this means an end to the relationship. It is okay to dissolve the relationship if either party is not comfortable with the present intended state of the relationship. Trying to persuade or coerce one another into something is toxic and will not bode well, no matter what you want to believe.

It is good to know that if we slow down the momentum of a relationship so everyone is on the same page, then whenever anything comes up that might change for one or the other, another meeting or conversation can be had. For example, when we meet with someone or a group of people one day, the logistics and information are defined in that moment, but as we each go about our lives in the days following that meeting, our ideas or thoughts may change. The best thing to do is to be in communication on a regular basis so that meaning doesn't get misunderstood down the road.

Chapter 10

Rapport

You can discover more about a person in an
hour of play than in a year of conversation.

—Plato

Rapport, by Merriam-Webster's definition, is "a friendly
relationship; relation marked by harmony, conformity, accord
or affinity." How you relate when you are connected with
yourself, family, friends, community, material, and nonphysical
things such as God is your rapport. How are you relating in
these connections?

Good, healthy rapport can be best described as being your
true, loving self while allowing others to be the same. You set
no conditions for others to be a certain way in order for you to
be happy, and vice versa.

Some key elements for successful rapport are

♦ eye contact,
♦ inclusive and open body language, and
♦ listening

The saying goes that when you look into the eyes of others, you can see their souls. That is so true. Have you ever looked into someone's eyes—really looked for a period of minutes—while discussing a topic? It truly breaks down barriers, and there is nothing hidden; your truths and their truths come out.

Body language is also essential in building rapport. If my arms are crossed in front of me, or my hands are on my hips, then I am sending a message that I am closed, that I do not regard someone's ideas as valuable, or that I do not want to hear that person's opinion. There is no hope for any good relationship to come about from closed or turned-off body language.

Another important aspect of body language is how people dress. When people dress in a way that covers so much of their bodies so that you can hardly see them (e.g., hats, sunglasses), it can be a distraction that gets in the way of building a solid foundation in the relationship.

> The biggest communication challenge is we don't listen to understand, we listen to reply.
>
> —Gabriel Garcia

I believe listening is the key to creating a positive rapport with someone. My paternal grandmother, Blanche, was my biggest role model for this attribute, and she taught me how to be a good listener. When I visited, Blanche would make tea, and we would pick out teacups, sit at her table, and visit. She would ask me how I was doing and then let me talk and share my life. All the while, she looked directly at me and absorbed every word and breath I took. These were very special moments; they seemed ethereal, as if angels were surrounding us, and we were the only ones in the entire world. The lesson

ANNE K. ROSS

I learned from these visits was that my grandmother was an amazing listener.

In my opinion, a relationship with great rapport is one in which there are deeply connected open hearts, open eyes, and open ears to the listening of the other.

Another key to successful rapport is the ability to listen without judgment or opinion. Focus solely on the other's words and body language to give you a sense of his or her true self. Sometimes a person simply wants to share information. If you have an opinion regarding what is being shared, it is important to ask if your opinion is wanted. When someone is seeking my advice, I like to turn the question back to the individual: "What do you think or feel?" Most of the time, people have already made up their minds and are seeking support. They want to know they are on the right track and need reassurance or acknowledgment that they and their opinions matter. It is my feeling that when people ask for advice, they are really trying to accept themselves fully and unconditionally, to know that they are loved.

When you come from a place of unconditional love (i.e., there are no conditions on your love), everything is joyous. Do you place conditions on your relationships? As you think about various relationships (personal, material, or spiritual), consider whether you have placed conditions on them in order for you to be happy. Be easy with your awareness and try to avoid being *judge-mental*—it's an interesting word when you look at it this way. You are trying to give yourself feedback so you can recognize feelings associated with these relationships.

♦ When you recognize that you *have* placed conditions on a relationship, ask yourself whether the relationship might be improved if you remove the conditions.

♦ If you have placed conditions on a relationship, and those conditions work for you, be aware that the relationship can become constrained in the future due to these conditions, because very rarely does anything stay stagnate. Everything and everyone is in constant change.

For example, let's say you fell in love with another person. At that specific moment in time, you were experiencing your true, authentic selves as perfect, whole, and complete. You basically fell in love with the *feeling* you get when you are in connection with that person. Outside conditions and personal circumstances are in a state of constant change, and over time the level or depth of your love will change unless you transform together on a similar path. Some of the conditions and circumstances that are in a constant state of change are as follows:

♦ work
♦ family
♦ finances
♦ an old belief system that doesn't serve you any longer

Maybe in the instant you fell in love with a person, you were really experiencing your love of God because of the pure connection; it's something to think about. Are you able to go with the flow and grow as a person? Do you expect someone or something to be a certain way in order for you to be happy? Be aware of what is going on and how you feel by your internal guidance system, the feeling and your interpretation of that feeling. Remember the body scan mentioned earlier?

Coaching can help you go from placing conditions on people in order to be happy to establishing relationships without conditions in order to live happily, content, and joy-filled.

It is also important to consider whether others are placing conditions on *you* in order for them to be happy. Do you have to be anything other than your true, authentic self in order for someone else to be happy? How does that make you feel?

Sometimes developing rapport is important because of work. It is necessary to have a collaborative relationship with someone or a group of people to function as a team. Communication is essential within any type of relationship, be it personal, social, or work. What is even more important is understanding the semantics when conversing with others. My meaning and your meaning of an idea might very well be the same, but we may disagree based on the language used. There are ideas, plans, and desires that are squelched because one or more people have to have their way using their words. It is good to note here that when this happens, someone is usually seeking to be in control, and in their "rightness;" regardless of whether everyone else is in agreement, the person will say that no one gets it or understands the meaning. This is all based upon his or her emotional survival belief, created long ago.

When there is any type of friction in the beginning, it is usually a matter of settling into normalcy. Some people are very competitive, driven, controlling, and high energy; they only see things their way, even if they say they are team players. In these instances, it is advantageous to go with the flow. Allow nature to take its course. Love them for their positive aspects, and keep focusing on these positive aspects while going with the flow. If you still feel you need to do something about it, ask them to go to lunch to get to know one another. Without being nosey, find out about their personal life to help you understand where they're coming from and why they think, behave, and say things that way.

More than likely, the people we have friction with are dealing with something or have created this behavior because of their pasts. When we take the time to get to know them, we can identify similarities and can usually help by being compassionate rather than making ourselves or others feel *wrong*. And, if for nothing else, to better acquaint ourselves with another.

Chapter 11

Goal Setting

What true patience is, is knowing that you want it and knowing that it's coming and actually enjoying the unfolding along the way. Understand that you never get it done. So, you might as well be patient. You never get it done, because every time you want and receive, you also receive a new perspective from which to want. Life is a constant unfolding of new desires and then a constant alignment to those desires.

—Abraham-Hicks

Goal setting is an important exercise, and it can be very enlightening when we achieve what we have set out to do. Here are a few guidelines I encourage you to consider when setting goals.

♦ Get excited! Raise up your energy to be in alignment with the goal you desire. Establishing a goal and being excited about it provides the correct energy (love) and creates the Law of Attraction in order to receive.

- Be realistic. If you set a goal of making $1 million but you've never made half of that goal, your goal is not realistic. Start by making smaller, more realistic goals. If you have made $250,000, set your goal for $500,000. If your goal is not realistic, it is not attainable.
- Goals should be measurable. Be clear and concise about specifics such as amount, a date, or any other details so that you know whether or not you've attained your goal. If you want to own a house with a specific style or in a specific neighborhood, list those details. When your goals are clear and specific, the universe will reciprocate.
- Act as if you have already achieved your goal. This is the most important of all strategies. If you say "I hope" or "maybe" or any other iffy words, the universe is going to provide you with an iffy response. Act like you are already in the position you want at work. Act like the million-dollar person you want to be. Act like the homeowner, builder, or writer that you desire for yourself. When you *feel* it within, keep that energy of feeling going. This is so important.
- Set short-term goals that will serve as milestones toward your big-picture goal. What do you plan to achieve at the three-month mark, the six-month mark, and beyond? Adjust these goals as needed.

Here are some examples of goals.

- "I will have an outline for a book by January 31, 2015. That book will be about healing and being happy, using the tools or toys that I practice and use on a daily basis to coach others."

- "I will achieve a 50 percent increase of profit in my business by December 21, 2015, through referrals by serving the greater good of all in a harmonious work environment, where my clients are eager, happy, and willing to collaborate and play."
- "I will lose thirty pounds by May 1, 2015, by eating healthy food whether I am at home or dining out, going to bed earlier, practicing positive affirmations, and surrounding myself with supportive people."

Stay focused on your goal, but do not be discouraged if it doesn't turn out exactly the way you wanted. Somewhere along the way, your ego may have thrown you a curveball. You may have become distracted, or your feeling did not match the goal. Pick up where you left off and get back on track. This is the best advice I can give you: stay focused on the feeling and the goal. Be persistent.

Keep making new goals. If you find yourself procrastinating to get started, make it a fun game. I create games for myself because then it is more fun, and it is easier to avoid becoming discouraged if I temporarily veer off track. Remember the steps above. Keep up with your breathing and meditation, and have fun.

In Closing

Don't look back! You're not going that way.

—Lily Ellis

There is never really a closing or ending of the journey. Keep the toys that you find helpful. Be easy with yourself. Be happy! Go find your happy place and share your authentic, true self with yourself and others.

I have included a list of suggested reading and meditation CDs in the appendix to continue your personal growth. They are all good in their own way, and you can start anywhere that pleases you. If you feel you would like a CD for meditation, choose one from the list or find one that sounds good to you. Start practicing on a daily basis and see where it takes you. You are meant to continually expand and grow. I also encourage you to watch Disney movies, Pixar movies, and any other movies in which creativity and imagination prevail. Grow in love, compassion, and happiness. Share that love, compassion, and happiness with yourself, and then share it with the world!

This book is based upon beliefs and philosophies that work for me. Use whatever resonates with you. The toys in this book are toys that I enjoy playing with every day, because they have helped me to learn, grow, and be happy.

When I look back, as I sometimes do, I see many experiences in which I calmly, happily, and peacefully sailed through with no negative triggers or intense ill will. I simply did what I needed to do for me at that specific moment to stay true to myself, even if it meant walking away without a word or cutting the cord. In those instances, I reaped the benefits of the toys. My health has improved dramatically. I have fun most of the day. Years ago this was not the case, and I am eternally grateful for doing the inner work, positive change and my expanding connection to God.

This is my wish for you: create the momentum of joy, creativity, playfulness, happiness, calm, and peace, and increase that momentum so that happy is your constant state of being.

I am so excited and grateful that you took the time and energy to read my book. My spiritual connection with God excites and amplifies my state of happiness. It is this belief that allows me to grow, expand, and receive the amazing gifts and manifestations that come into my life every day. I see you achieving the same.

Now, go and get your happy on!

Blessings,

Anne K. Ross

Appendix
Suggested Resources

A Course In Miracles: Foundation for Inner Peace, Combined Volume, Third Edition. Dr. Helen Schucman. Mill Valley: Foundation for Inner Peace, 2007.

A Return to Love: Reflections on the Principles of "A Course in Miracles." Marianne Williamson. New York: HarperCollins, 1992.

Angels of Abundance: Heaven's 11 Messages to Help You Manifest Support, Supply, and Every Form of Abundance. Doreen Virtue and Grant Virtue. Carlsbad: Hay House, 2014.

The Art and Science of Raja Yoga. Swami Kriyananda. Nevada City: Crystal Clarity. 2010.

Autobiography of a Yogi. Parmahansa Yogananda. Nevada City: Crystal Clarity. 1993.

The Book of Awakening: Having the Life You Want by Being Present to the Life You Have. Mark Nepo. York Beach: Conari Press, 2000.

Change Your Thoughts—Change Your Life: Living the Wisdom of the Tao. Dr. Wayne W. Dyer. Carlsbad: Hay House, 2007.

Co-creating at its Best: A Conversation Between Master Teachers. Dr. Wayne W. Dyer and Esther Hicks. Carlsbad: Hay House, 2014.

Codependent No More: How to Stop Controlling Others and Start Caring for Yourself. Melody Beattie. Center City: Hazelden, 1986.

Excuses Begone!: How to Change Lifelong, Self-Defeating Thinking Habits. Dr. Wayne W. Dyer. Carlsbad: Hay House, 2009.

Getting into the Vortex: Guided Meditations CD and User Guide. Esther Hicks and Jerry Hicks. Carlsbad: Hay House, 2014.

Gift of Change: Spiritual Guidance for Living Your Best Life. Marianne Williamson. New York: Perfect Bound/HarperCollins, 2004.

God is For Everyone. Swami Kriyananda. Nevada City: Crystal Clarity, 2003.

The Heart of the Soul: Emotional Awareness. Gary Zukav and Linda Francis. New York: Free Press, 2001.

The Law of Attraction: The Basics of the Teaching of Abraham. Ester Hicks and Jerry Hicks.

The Law of Success: Using the Power of Spirit to Create Health, Prosperity, and Happiness. Parmahansa Yogananda Nevada City: Crystal Clarity,

The Little Book of Bleeps: "Ponder These for Awhile!" Quotations from the Movie What the Bleep Do We Know!? William Arntz and Betsy Chasse, editors. Beyond Words Publishing.

Love without Conditions. Paul Ferrini. Greenfield: Heartways Press, 1994.

Loving What Is: Four Questions That Can Change Your Life. Byron Katie. New York: Random House, 2002.

My Stroke of Insight: A Brain Scientist's Personal Journey. Dr. Jill Bolte Taylor. New York: Penguin Publishing, 2008.

Namaste Meditation CD. Namaste.

The Purpose Driven Life: What on Earth Am I Here For? Rick Warren. Grand Rapids: Zondervan, 2002.

Relax: Soothing Sounds for Mind and Spirit Meditation CD. Bath & Body Works.

The Science of Mind: A Philosophy, a Faith, a Way to Live. Ernest Holmes. New York: Penguin Putnam, 1938.

The Secret of Letting Go. Guy Finlay. Woodbury: Llewellyn Publications, 2007.

The Spirit of Yoga Meditation CD. Ben Leinbach.

The Spontaneous Fulfillment of Desire. Deepok Chopra. New York: Harmony Books, 2003.

The Way of Mastery. Jeshua. Ashland: Shanti Christo, 2005.

Think and Grow Rich. Napoleon Hill. North Hollywood: Wilshire Book Co., 1999.

The Untethered Soul: The Journey beyond Yourself. Michael S. Singer. Oakland: New Harbinger Publications, 2007.

What You Think of Me Is None of My Business. Dr. Terry Cole-Whittaker. New York: Penguin Publishing, 1979.

Wishes Fulfilled: Mastering the Art of Manifesting. Dr. Wayne W. Dyer. Carlsbad: Hay House, 2012.

It Works: The Famous Little Red Book That Makes Your Dreams Come True! R. H. Jarrett. BN Publishing, 2008.

You Can Heal Your Life. Louise Hay. Carlsbad: Hay House, 1987.

Zen Garden Meditation CD. Kokin Gumi.